The New Low Carb Guide for Beginners

70 Delicious Ketogenic Diet Recipes

Table of content

Part III – Low Carb Casseroles

Chapter 1 – Chicken Casserole Recipes

Part IV – Low Carb Meals: Top-20 Quick&Easy Delicious Low Carb Recipes To Lose Weight Fast

Introduction

Hundreds of different diets are available with their benefits and drawbacks. The majority of these foods requires you to eat fewer calories than the requirement of your body. It is important for you to eat fewer calories and burn more to shed some pounds. Unfortunately, everyone is different, and their reasons behind obesity are also different. Before following any diet, it is essential to understand the working pattern of your body and know the effects of food on your body. For successful reduction in weight, you should eat the right food and select a regular workout to force your body to melt excessive fat. With the help of diet and exercise, you have to break the fat reserves of your body.

Low carb diet is famous all around the world to reduce weight, and this has been in existence for various years. The basic aim of this diet is to discourage the consumption of processed food. You have to provide essential vitamins, minerals, and nutrients to your body by eating whole foods. Your body requires a particular amount of nutrients to remain healthy. Fats, fiber, carbohydrates, and protein are essential elements for the health of your body. Protein is the building block for each cell in your body. It is essential to repair and build cells. Proteins are made of amino acids, and there are 12 essential amino acids for your body for healthy growth and development.

Unfortunately, many of these important amino acids can ' t be made naturally in your body. You need protein to get these amino acids for bones and blood. Carbohydrates are necessary to provide energy to your body. There are several types of carbohydrates, such as complex and simple. Both types have good and bad carbs. Carbohydrates are the primary source of fuel for your body. They turned into glucose and your body cells will burn them for energy. If there is no available supply of carbohydrates, your body will burn fat to get energy. The low carb diet works on this principle to let your body burn fat to provide energy to the organs.

The most important principle of the low-carb diet is to reduce the number of carbohydrates in your diet. It will force your body to burn fat to get energy for cells and organs. Once you started following a low carb diet, your body will switch to fat burning mode after 3 to 4 days. Protein and stored fat will provide energy to your body. This process is known as ketosis, and it is a powerful way to burn your body fat. High protein and low-fat diet will reduce the risk of diabetes, heart disease, and epilepsy. Read more about this diet.

Part I - Chapter 1: Low Carb 101: Low Carb Diet - Proven Way to Lose 15 Lbs (7 KG) in Two-Week Challenge Without Even Trying

Chapter 1 – Carb Cycling for Weight Loss

Carb cycling is an important method of dieting that involves a particular plan to increase and decrease carbohydrate intake. You have to increase or decrease your caloric intake as well. There are various protocols for carb cycling, but the most suggested are as under:

High-carb Days

These days require you to include 2 – 2.5 grams carbs for one pound of your body weight. These are higher regarding your calorie intake.

Low-carb Days

Most protocols dowel your intake almost 0.5 grams of carbohydrates for one pound of your body weight. These days can be difficult for you, especially with regular weight training. Calorie intake will be lower than your highcarb days.

No-carb Days

During these days, you can take less than 30 grams of carbohydrates for your whole day. During these days, you have to reduce your caloric consumption as well.

In short, carb cycling requires you to pay close attention to meal planning and strictly adhere to it.

Does carb cycling work?

The concept of carb cycling came from bodybuilding industry because the trainers were used to experiment with their carbs to reduce fat layers of their body. When any person pulls carbohydrates from his/her diet for an extended period, he/she can reduce weight. The longer deprivation of carbohydrates can decrease the metabolism rate of your body. As you reintroduce carbs, the body rebounds and hold every bit of sugar, water and carb. To avoid this situation, you can get the advantage of carb cycling. With the help of carb cycling, your body will not deprive of carbs to reduce the speed of metabolism of your body.

Your body may experience a catabolic fat burning state on your low carb period. The high carb time act as boost period to increase your metabolism and the low carb days serve as a fat burning period.

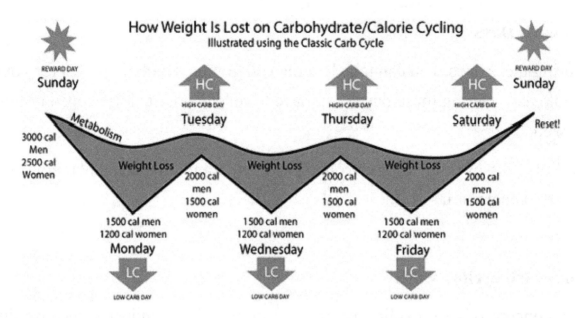

For the best physical and mental health, you can follow 12-week carb cycle. Consumption of excessive carb can increase your insulin level and trigger ability of your body to store fat. With carb cycling, you can balance the use of carbohydrates on a regular basis. High carb days are essential for your hormones that affect the metabolism of muscle protein and energy expenditure, such as cortisol, testosterone, and insulin. By refilling glycogen stores, you can maintain the intensity of your workout. The no-carb and lowcalorie days are good to ramp up your fat burning speed. You can use the carb cycling procedure to build muscle and reduce the chances of fat storage in your body.

Chapter 2 – Tips to Get Started with Carb Cycling

Carb cycling is a brilliant strategy to reduce weight without affecting the speed of your metabolism. Low carb diet doesn ' t mean to quit the consumption of carbs altogether. Healthy carbs are essential for your body to rev up your metabolism. You should stick to vegetable and proteins on a regular basis. Carb cycling routine can be different for everyone; therefore, it is important to find a right formula for you. There are a few tips for you to get started with carb cycling:

Choose a Right Formula

You will need a typical schedule to alternate between high and low-carb days almost 6 times in one week. You can enjoy a reward meal on the 7th day. You can change a set up for one week by your fitness objectives. For instance, if you want to reduce weight, you have to aim for 5 low-carb days with 2 high-carb days.

On the other hand, if you want to gain weight and muscle, you can include 4 to 5 high-carb days. You have to keep an exact balance between low-carb and high-carb days. There should be a particular space between both periods. Closely monitor your progress and adjust your carb cycling schedule to see the best results.

Select Your Fuel

Low-carb days don't mean to munch only white meat and eat pasta in the remaining days. There are whole grains, fruits, and legumes to consume during high-carb days. You can include fruits in your diet to get high-quality protein. These fruits will keep you energized throughout your day, while promoting weight loss. During your low-carb period, you can eat fish, chicken, lean beef, tofu, and eggs. Load up your diet with fresh fruits and vegetables.

Healthy Snacks

Lots of professional trainers often suggest having one cheat day. The weekly reward is not a good option for those who want to reduce the maximum amount of weight. Some people may end up eating more than 5,000 calories in one cheat day. This cheat day can spoil all your efforts, but don't worry and get the advantage of healthy snacks. You can enjoy a bowl of cereal with extra fruit and other healthy meals on your cheat day. If you want to eat something special, prepare it at home and keep an eye on the calories of this meal.

Carb Cycling Meal Plan

If you are trying to reduce weight, it is essential to remove all unhealthy ingredients and processed food from your pantry. It doesn't mean to eat them all, but you can gift them to your friends and relatives. To reduce weight, a woman should plan her diet around 1,200 and the males around 1,500 during low-carb days. You can slightly increase this limit during the high-carb period. You should calculate the perfect portion of every macronutrient by getting a particular number of grams for each pound of your body weight.

Carb Cycling Limit for Men

If your weight is 200 lbs:

High-carb Day: 400 grams carbs and 200 grams protein, reduce fat consumption as little as possible

Low-carb Day: 100 grams carbs, 250 grams protein and 250 grams fat

Carb Cycling Limit for Women

If your weight is 200 lbs:

High-carb Day: 200 grams carbs and 150 grams protein, reduce fat consumption as little as possible

Low-carb Day: 40 grams carbs, 200 grams protein and 20 grams fat

For both low and high carb days, make sure to eat your breakfast early in the morning and divide remaining calories between 4 to 6 meals throughout your day.

Low-carb Meal Plan

Carb Cycling
Low-Carb Day Meal Plan

Breakfast (7 a.m.)
- [ ] 2 scrambled eggs
- [ ] 1/2 bell pepper

Morning Snack (10 a.m.)
- [ ] protein shake
- [ ] berries

Lunch (1 p.m.)
- [ ] 3 oz. grilled chicken
- [ ] 1 cup asparagus

Afternoon Snack (4 p.m.)
- [ ] 1/3 cup oatmeal
- [ ] 10 almonds

Dinner (7 p.m.)
- [ ] 3 oz. steak
- [ ] 2 cups steamed broccoli or cauliflower

High-carb Meal Plan

Carb Cycling
High-Carb Day Meal Plan

Breakfast (7 a.m.)

☐ 1/2 cup oatmeal
☐ walnuts and berries

Morning Snack (10 a.m.)

☐ apple
☐ 2 tablespoons peanut or almond butter

Lunch (1 p.m.)

☐ 1/2 turkey sandwich on whole-wheat bread

Afternoon Snack (4 p.m.)

☐ 1 cup three-bean salad
☐ 1 cup quinoa

Dinner (7 p.m.)

☐ 3 oz. grilled chicken
☐ 1 cup whole-wheat pasta and pesto

Formula to Calculate Consumption of Protein, Fat and Carbs

Formula for Men: **High-carb day**

> 2 to 3 grams carbs multiply by your body weight
>
> 1 to 1.25 grams protein multiply by your body weight
>
> Reduce fat in your diet as much as you can **Low-carb day**

> (0.5 to 1.5 grams carbs) X (your body weight)
>
> (1.25 to 1.5 grams protein) X (your body weight)
>
> (0.15 to 0.35 grams fat) X (your body weight)

Women

High-carb day

>(Almost 1 gram carbs) X (your body weight)

>(0.75 grams protein) X (your body weight)

>Reduce consumption of fat as much as you can **Low-carb**

day

>(0.2 to 0.5 grams carbs) X (your body weight)

>(Almost 1 gram protein) X (your body weight)

>(0.1 to 0.2 grams fat) X (your body weight)

Chapter 3 – Low Carb Diet Plan to Reduce Weight

Low carb diet will help you to reduce a right amount of weight because of the fundamental principle behind it. This diet is quite different than fad diets because you have to cut carbs in your diet to melt excessive fat of your body.

Eat Whole and Natural Foods

Whole foods are better than processed food item because these are available in the natural state with all nutrition. The whole grains come with endosperm, bran and germ layers. The crushed grains are better than processed foods. The natural food should be free from all chemicals and artificial ingredients and contain all nutrients and have not gone through any chemical process and synthetic ingredient. The whole foods are good for your body because these contain all nutrients to provide the original value of food to the body.

Prefer Unrefined Foods over Refined

Refined food items are not good for your health because these are processed foods and have no original nutrients. These foods usually go through a particular procedure to enhance their taste and increase their shelf life. This process can improve the texture and taste of food, but make it unhealthy as well. The refined sugar is not healthy, and it is often preferred to buy brown sugar to use in your coffee and tea.

You can also notice the use of white sugar in the baking recipes because it can give a smooth texture to your pastry and cake. It will be good to use brown sugar instead to provide complete nutrients to your food. You should prefer unrefined ingredients instead of refined food items.

Increase the Use of Fruits and Vegetables

You can notice a common thing in all diet plans that they promote the use of fresh fruit and vegetables for better health. Healthy nutrients of fresh fruit and vegetables are the main reason behind them because your body requires minerals, vitamins, and fiber that keep you feel full for longer time. Make sure to eat fruits and vegetables come directly from the farmer ' s market or buy them from stall instead of using frozen fruits and vegetables.

Avoid Saturated Fats

There is no need to afraid of the fat in general because the healthy fat is also required for the HDL cholesterol of the body. You can enjoy dairy foods and meat to get good cholesterol, and the clean eating means to eliminate bad fat from your diet and take good fat that is essential for your health. Try to focus on the healthy fats that are available in the form of canola oil, olive oil, fish, and nuts.

Reduce the Sodium Consumption

It is recommended to take only 2,300 mg sodium on a regular basis and to lose weight, the people try to limit this consumption to 1,000 mg, but it is useless. They consume fast and processed foods that have lots of sodium and sugar. If you want to limit the consumption of sodium, make sure to eat homemade food and prepare your meal without increasing salt because lots of other spices and herbs are also available to enhance the taste of your meal.

Eat Less Meat

Meat contains saturated fat that is not good for your health, but it is not possible to cut it completely from your diet. The meat is an excellent source of protein, and it is important to include meat in your diet. There are lots of options to eat meat in a healthy way, such as instead of consuming deep fried chicken in dinner, you can use bits of chicken in the healthy soup.

Skip High-Calorie Drinks

Soft drinks are filled with carbohydrates, salt, and sugar that are bad for your health. Avoid soft drinks and prefer plain water. You can start your morning with skimmed milk, tea without sugar and fresh fruit juice.

Divide you Food into Several Small Meals

Low-carb diet prompts people to divide their large portion into several small meals. It is quite impressive to take five to six small meals instead of taking two to three large meals. Make every meal at the right time, and don ' t skip meals because it may urge you to overeat. You can enjoy healthy snacks between meals to avoid overeating and stabilize the energy for the whole day.

Reduce Your Alcohol Consumption

If you are addicted to alcohol, then don ' t cut it completely, just reduce its consumption. It will be good to get rid of this habit. Limit your consumption to one drink in a day if you are a woman. A man can take almost two drinks in a day. Excessive use of alcohol is not good for your health because it can be the reason of dehydration and promote obesity by increasing calories in your diet.

Reduce Your Sugar Ingestion

Not only sodium, but the sugar is also bad for your health. If you want to reduce weight, it is important to reduce your sugar ingestion. It is recommended to take nine teaspoons of sugar in a day for men and six teaspoons in a day for women. The baked items, candies, and sodas are sugary foods, so avoid them entirely. Healthy alternatives are available in the form of yogurt, cereal, tomato sauce, etc.

A low-carb diet is ultimately beneficial for you because it can provide all essential nutrients to your body to boost your energy. There are lots of elements, including vitamin, iron, B-complex, magnesium, calcium and others that are essential for the proper functions of your body cells. A lowcarb diet can promote your health by regulating the sugar level in the bloodstream and provide you steady energy for the whole day. If you want to enjoy all these benefits, you should trim down the consumption of refined foods and sweets.

Chapter 4 – Proven Ways to Lose 15 Lbs in Two Weeks

If you want to reduce 15 pounds in two weeks, you have to make any necessary changes in your diet. It is essential to consult a doctor to get a suitable diet plan for your goal:

Drink Water

To reduce weight, you have to flush out toxins from your system. Water has zero calories; therefore, you should prefer plain water over sugary drinks. If you can limit yourself to water, you can increase the speed of weight loss. You can enjoy unsweetened tea or green tea with lemon to enjoy flavored drinks. Feel free to drink a cup of coffee without milk or always use skimmed milk. Water can increase your metabolism and help you feel full for longer. As per recent studies (Brenda Davy), two glasses of chilled water can increase your metabolism up to 40 percent for almost 15 to 20 minutes. Participants of this study reduce 15 pounds in three months by drinking water only.

Cut Junk Food from Your Diet

Completely cut junk food from your diet to reduce weight in a short period. Stay away fatty and greasy food items with a high content of sugar. If you want to eat granola bars and yogurt, carefully check their labels to consumption of extra sugar. Some flavored yogurt and granola bars can be filled with sugar.

Stay Away from Whtie Carbs

Everything from cookies to pasta is full of carbohydrates. These carbohydrates are sugar in camouflage. These are villains to spike your fat stores, insulin levels and increase your body weight. To reduce insulin spike, you should cut the processed carbs from your diets, such as bread, potatoes, and rice. Moreover, donuts, cookies, ice cream, cakes, and pretzels should be cut from your diet.

If you want to reduce 20 pounds in two weeks, you should say goodbye to white carbohydrates. To start ketosis phase of your body, try to reduce consumption of fat and carbohydrates. Switch your body to a low-carb diet and completely cut starchy vegetables, such as squash, carrots, potatoes, and whole grains (brown rice and quinoa) and fruits with sugar (apples, bananas, and oranges). Fill your refrigerator and pantry with healthy food items to reduce the chances of unhealthy cravings.

Negative Calorie Foods

Negative calorie food items are actually negative, and these foods require more energy to digest food. These food items will not increase your calorie count. There are a few negative calorie vegetables, such as beet-root, cabbage, asparagus, broccoli, celery, cauliflower, garlic, cucumber, lettuce, green beans, radish, onion, zucchini, turnip, and spinach.

If you want to consume fruits, you can eat cranberries, blueberries, grapefruit, cantaloupe, lemons, honeydew, oranges, lime, papayas, raspberries, tangerines, strawberries, watermelon and tomatoes.

Lean Proteins and Vegetables

Instead of pork and beef, you can consume leaner meals, such as chicken and fish. To provide fatty acids and omega oil to your body, you can consume fish. The chicken meat is full of protein; therefore, it will help you to reduce a right amount of weight. You can prepare chicken soup with vegetables and fish with boiled vegetables. It will fill your body with protein and fiber.

Low-carb Diet

Instead of going after fad diets, you can consider a low-carb diet. Before starting a low-carb diet, it will be good to follow a short-term fad diet. Initially, you have to cleanse your body with liquid-based diet. Increase the consumption of fresh juices of fruits and vegetables. A liquid diet of 7 days will help you to flush toxins out of your body. Detox diet offers quick result, but you shouldn't follow them for a longer period.

Change Your Eating Routine

Low-calorie diet doesn't mean to stay away from food. You will eat your regular meals, but reduce their size. Prolonged fasting can increase the chances of muscle loss. You should eat all your meals, but use small plates and spoons to feel full and satisfied. Instead of half-filling a big plate, you can use a small plate.

Set a Time for Eating

To successfully reduce a right amount of weight, you should set a timetable for eating. Strictly follow this schedule and always eat at a particular time. You shouldn ' t eat something heavy in the night. Try to finish your meal at least two hours before going to bed. Some people eat food in front of the TV; therefore, they eat mindlessly without realizing the taste of food. You should switch off your TV or any other program, and pay complete attention to your food. Enjoy each bite of your food and keep your internet and mobile away from you while eating.

Zero Water Retention

If you want to reduce water retention in your body, then it is important to decrease salt consumption because the excessive sodium in your body can be the reason for fluid retention. Reduce the amount of salt from your food and you will be able to enjoy zero water retention.

Search for Hidden Calories

If you are trying to reduce weight, it is important to prevent hidden calories because these can ruin your weight loss efforts.

- You need to be very careful while selecting between doughnut and bagel. The doughnut might have lower calories than a bagel.

- If you want to eat a muffin, focus on its size because the size can increase or decrease the calories.

- Select your salad wisely because some fatty dressing can make your salad unhealthy. It may lead you to increase weight instead of shedding some pounds.

- It will be good to explore different salad toppings and check their calorie count before using them.

- Sugary drinks can make your fatty; therefore, prefer green tea instead of creamy coffee or sweet tea.

- Control your portion and eat on a smaller plate. Avoid beer because it can increase your body weight.

Replacement of Unhealthy Meals

There are lots of meals that can dramatically increase your weight and you may even ignore these things. The followings are some alternatives that you should consider reducing weight:

- Replace baked popcorns with simple one without butter and cheese.

- The candy can increase the weight so prefer dry fruits.

- Casual chocolate bars should be replaced with organic black chocolates.

- Cake or any other item from a bakery can increase your weight, so replace it with banana bread made at home.

- There is no need to consume French fries because these may contain 500 to 600 calories. Replacing French fries with sweet potatoes will be good.

- Replace calorie rich energy drinks with plain water or lemon water.

- Sugary cereals should be replaced with oatmeal.

Frame Your Cheating Days

Cheat days are critical in your diet; therefore, you should carefully plan your cheat days, such as:

- Start your day with plenty of water.

- Do your regular workout.

- Start your day with a healthy breakfast.

- Select a cheat meal for your lunch.

- Go for an evening walk to burn calories.

- You can also enjoy a cheat meal in the night, but make sure to avoid wheat grains and other heavy meals in the evening.

Shop with a List

If you want to save your money and time, then it is important to prepare a list of items that you want to buy. This list should be free from unhealthy food items because the existence of unhealthy foods can force you to go for injurious craving. You should buy only healthy meals and stuff your refrigerator with fresh fruits and vegetables.

Pack Your Food with Protein

If you want to reduce weight at a fast speed, then you should include protein in your food items. Your diet should have egg white, chicken, low-fat yogurt and skimmed milk to include sufficient protein in your diet.

K.I.S.S (Keep it Simple and Sweet)

KISS is a simple formula to change your diet and eating habits. You need to keep your food simple and sweet. There are numerous options for you, but you should reduce complications from your diet. Initially, include simple workouts and diet plans in your routine to increase your motivation. Your weight loss goals should be realistic and achievable to avoid any demoralization.

Distract Your Taste Buds

If you are trying to lose weight, you have to relax instead of starving for food. Prepare a diet schedule and include balanced meals in your diet. If you feel bored or demoralized, then you can distract your taste buds. Keep altering your meal plans, such as in the first 15 days; you can consume fresh fruits, vegetables, and grilled chicken, and after 15 days, you can consume grilled fish, soups and sandwiches.

Chapter 5 – Workout to Burn Maximum Fat

There are some good exercises that you should try to reduce weight and get better results in 21 days:

Pushups

Push ups are great to reduce a right amount of weight and build muscle. You can challenge your core muscles, forearms and rotator cuffs with the help of this exercise. Put your hands on floor and lower your body until your chest touches the floor. Push your body back to the starting position. See the images above to get an idea of this exercise.

Spiderman Lunges

It is simple, just follow the steps below:

• Put your right knee on the floor and bring your left foot forward and flat on the floor.

• Lean frontward and put both hands level on the floor along with your left foot.

• Lean frontward even more and hold this position for a few seconds.

• Switch position of legs and replicate for almost 5 to 10 times. See the image above.

Up-down Plank

Set your position on your forearms while keeping your palm on the floor.
Keep your left hand inside under your shoulders and press your body upward.
Move your other hand, in a plank position with the straight arm. See the
above give picture to practice this post.

Lateral Lunges

Start it by standing on your feet with hands on hips and step out the right while shifting your body weight from the right leg to form 90 degree angle and then shift it to the left leg in a similar way. You can hold weights in your hands. See the image above.

Jump Squats

Cross your arms on the chest and keep your head up with a straight back. Set your feet at the shoulder width and keep your back straight and squat down while you inhale. Keep your upper thighs parallel to the flower. Exert force at the balls of your feet and jump up in the air as high as possible. Your thighs will play the role of spring. See the image above.

Mountain Climbers

It is a full body workout, and numerous muscles may work on this exercise, such as biceps, triceps, oblique, lower Trapezius, quadriceps, hip, hamstrings, etc. Start this with pushup position, and your hands and toes will support your weight. Flex the knee and hips and bring one leg to an approximate position. It will be a starting position, now explosively reverse your legs at the same situation. See the image above.

Bodyweight Sit Through

Start with your hands and knees and rise up on your toes and make your core firm. Rotate your body by moving your left hand up to your chest and push your leg through the available space under your body. You can reverse these steps as per as you feel comfortable. You can rotate your both legs, one by one, and given above picture will give you an idea of this exercise.

Ice Skaters

Start this exercise by standing on one leg and hop from side to side. Switch your legs while hoping and swing your arms while touching opposite legs. See the above image.

Prone Cobra

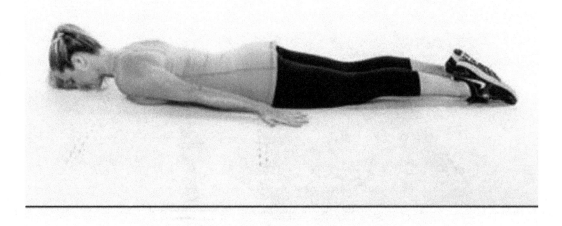

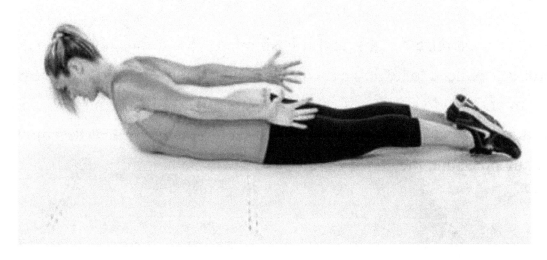

It is an endurance exercise that enables you to make your belly flat. Just lie down while keeping your stomach horizontal on the floor. Spread your hands on the floor while lying on the floor. Above image will help you to understand the posture.

Skinny Dip

It is a great exercise for abs, and it is simple to do at your house. To do this exercise, you need to lie down on the floor on the left side and proper up your left arm and bend your knees at a 90-degree angle. Lift the hip off the floor and raise the bent right leg almost a few feet. You can repeat this move for the both sides, and the above-given picture will be helpful.

PartII – Low Carb Soups

If you are looking for some really efficient and quick ways to lose weight, the best thing is to go on a low carb diet that helps you avoid all the starch and sugar so that you can stop eating things that only pile up weight and cause trouble in the long run.

By taking in a low carb diet, you can eat all you want and feel satisfied as there is no need to give up real food. You can eat as much protein, natural fats and fruits and vegetables that you like. These low carb diets just work great, and there are hundreds and thousands of success stories that have proved how effective how they have been.

Having a low carb diet means that you get to eat lesser carbohydrates and limit your intake of sugars and starches that cause hunger and lead to weight gain. This is an excellent way to diet as you can eat all that yummy food you love and still lose weight. Recent studies have shown that low-carb diet is both easy to follow and helps you get rid of excessive weight and controls the blood sugar levels, keeping it from going above the recommended range.

When it comes to going ahead with the low carb diet, there is also a god variety of meal plans that you can choose and low carb soups are an excellent way to satisfy your hunger and achieve the targeted weight loss.

The best thing about having soups is that contain all the right ingredients like chicken stock, chicken pieces, and vegetables, but they are free of all types of fats that are harmful to out body. Chicken stock only contains fats that are good for health and are consumed by the body very quickly, and they keep you satisfied for longer periods of time as they are full of foods that take a longer time to break up.

It is all about making the right choices to remain fit and healthy and low carb soups are the best that can help you eat well and live a good life without actually making nay sacrifice.

Chapter 01: Low Carb Vegetable Soups

When you begin your low carb diet and look forward to losing weight by eliminating all carbohydrates, it is necessary that you take things easy and feel satisfied in the beginning because if you feel ravenous and unable to control yourself, the purpose of dieting will fail. Eating enough on a low carb diet means that any fats that you eat will get burned by the body as fuel and the levels of fat storing hormones will go down. This way, you will become a fat burning machine as your body will lose weight without starvation or food deprivation.

To make your low carb diet work the best way and yield most useful results, eating vegetable soups is a great way to get your daily dose of vegetables. However, it is necessary that you keep the carbohydrates level low and do not buy just any soup of the supermarket rack but check out which vegetable soup offers the least carbohydrates. The best thing would be to make soup on your own using the freshest of vegetables that give a great taste and provide the right blend of calories required at this time.

Another great way to make things work is that you can make a big pot of soup and enjoy them during the weekdays when you do not have time to make them at leisure. There are so many good and healthy vegetables to choose from the list of foods that you can have during your low carb diet plan and use them in the soup for great taste as well as a healthy addition to the meal.

Some of the best vegetables that are low in carbohydrate include:

- Spinach

- Button mushrooms

- Snap peas

- Bell peppers

- Celery

You need to know that many vegetables have low carb content while others contain lots of carbohydrates. When making a low carb vegetable soup, it is necessary to remember that you must choose vegetables that contain low levels of carb so that they fill you up most efficiently and reduce the intake of carbs for better results.

This chapter brings you some 5 great recipes of low carb vegetable soups that will help to begin your diet with some of the most delicious foods.

Recipe no. 1 - Low Carb Healthy Slow-Cooked Vegetable Soup

Ingredients

1 medium zucchini cubed

4 cloves garlic, chopped

2 stalks celery, diced

1 cups frozen broccoli

3 medium carrots, sliced

½ small parsnip, sliced

2 large onions, chopped

1 tbsp. salt

1/4 cup tomato paste

5 cups water

1 tbsp. olive oil

A dash of red pepper flakes for flavor

How to Prepare

Begin the cooking process by sautéing onions in the olive oil. Add all the vegetables one by one and follow with seasoning and tomato paste. Stir everything together so that it is all mixed well and fill the pot with water. Also, add salt and red pepper flakes or you can leave them for the end depending on how you want to do it.

Bring the contents a boil and lower the heat and leave the soup to simmer for 3 to 4 hours. It will get ready on low flame and taste awesome. You can add croutons to enjoy with this yummy tasting soup.

Recipe no. 2 - Low Carb Moroccan Chickpea Soup
Ingredients

2 tbsp. olive oil

2 medium onions chopped

4 celery sticks, chopped

4 tsp ground cumin

1.5-litre hot vegetable stock

800g chopped plum tomatoes

800g can chickpeas, rinsed and drained

200g frozen broad beans

Zest and juice of ½ lemon

A little garlic

Coriander or parsley for serving

Flatbread optional

How to Cook

Heat oil in a big pot and fry onions and celery for almost 10 minutes till they both are soft, make sure to keep stirring so that they do not stick to the bottom. Put in cumin and continue frying for at least another minute.

Turn up the heat and add the vegetable stock, tomatoes and chickpeas as well black pepper and bring to a boil. Once the stock is fully boiled, turn down the flame and let it simmer. After a short while, add the broad beans and lemon juice and let it cook. Add seasonings and let them cook for a short while.

Add garlic, lemon juice and chopped herbs. The Moroccan chickpea soup is ready for serving.

Recipe no. 3 - Carrot & Coriander soup Ingredients

2tbsp. vegetable oil

2 onions, chopped

2 tsp ground coriander

2 potatoes chopped

900g carrots peeled and chopped

1.5 liters vegetable stock

Handful of coriander for garnish

How to Make

Heat oil in a big pan and add onions. Fry them till they are soft, it will take approximately 5 minutes. Add the ground coriander and potatoes and cook for a minute. Then put in carrots and the stock and bring them to boil.

Reduce the heat and cover the pot. Leave it to cook for at least 20 to thirty minutes till the potatoes and carrots are really tender. Remove from heat and let it cool a bit and put in the food processor along with the coriander. Grind to a smooth paste, return to pan and add salt, pepper, and seasoning as you like them.

Reheat the soup and it is ready to serve.

Recipe no. 4 - Indian Chickpea & Vegetable Soup
Ingredients

2 tbsp. vegetable oil

2 medium sized onions chopped

2 tsp finely grated ginger

2 garlic clove chopped

2 tbsp. all mixed spice

1.5 liters vegetable stock

4 medium sized carrots chopped in pieces

800g chickpeas

200g green beans chopped coarsely

Salt as per your taste

Seasonings like bay leaf, celery salt, curry powder and Italian seasoning

How to Cook

Heat oil in a pan and add onion, ginger, and garlic. Fry them for 2 minutes and add the allspice mix so that it gets coated on the vegetables really well. Add the stock and carrots and let them cook on medium heat for at least 10 minutes.

Add the chickpeas too and whizz up the soup a bit with the help of a stick blender. Put in the beans too and let the concoction simmer on low heat for a few minutes. A great tasting low carb vegetable soup is ready for serving. It can be eaten with bread or croutons and will taste just divine.

Recipe no. 5 - Leek, Fennel, and Broccoflower soup
Ingredients

2 tablespoon olive oil

2 leeks, trimmed, thinly sliced

2 large fennel bulbs, trimmed, halved, thinly sliced

4 cloves garlic, thinly sliced

1 big broccoflower, cut into small florets

1 liter vegetable stock

1 bay leaf

Salt & freshly ground black pepper

1 cup extra light sour cream

Crusty bread for serving

How to Cook

Heat oil in a big pan and add leek, fennel and garlic cooking over low heat for about 10 minutes or until they are soft. Add the broccoflower, bay leaf, and stock and cook till it boils. Cover the lid and leave to simmer for about 10 to 15 minutes till the broccoflower is all soft.

Take the pan off from flame and blend it in a food process till it becomes smooth and add seasoning. Before serving put in a little sour cream with a spoon in the center of the bowl and grind some fresh black pepper for an amazing taste.

The soup is ready to be presented with crusty bread.

Chapter 02: Chicken Soup Recipes

Chicken soup is one of the most liked appetizers and meals all over the world. Children and adults love to enjoy a hot bowl of chicken soup when they feel a little under the weather or even when they want to have something light or delicious that can make them feel happy.

If you are looking for ways to cut down on your intake of carbs and want to eat something that is nutritious and at the same time filling, then the chicken soup is perhaps the best option. Not only it is tasty and filling, but it helps you eat the right way and lose excessive weight without starving yourself.

This chapter brings some really nutritious and easy to make low carb chicken soup recipes that will help you enjoy a new variety of chicken soup every day. These recipes are the best, easy to put together and offer carb free delicacies for you to enjoy.

Recipe no. 1 – Low Carb Authentic Chicken Soup
Ingredients

1 tsp pepper

2 tsp rosemary

1 tsp sage

2 tsp sea salt

32 oz. chicken breast diced

8 cups chicken broth

2 cup cauliflower

4 tbsp. celery

1 cup chopped onion

How to Make

Chop all the ingredients and combine them in a pot and leave to cook for at least 2 to 4 hours so that the chicken, as well as cauliflower and the seasonings, get mixed really well and give off a very delicious aroma.

When you feel the soup is ready, add salt and pepper to taste. If you want to add some cream to it for better flavor, add 1 teaspoon of low fat cream after pouring it into the bowl and it will just taste extraordinary.

Recipe no. 2 - Thai Chicken & Mushroom Broth
Ingredients

2-liter hot chicken stock

2 tbsp. Thai red curry paste

2 tbsp. Thai fish sauce

4 tsp sugar

Zest and juice of 2 approximately limes

200g sliced Portobello mushrooms

A bunch of sliced spring onions, separate the whites and greens

400g leftover shredded chicken

How to Prepare

Put the chicken stock in a pan and add the curry paste, fish sauce, sugar, lime juice and most of the zest while saving a little for garnish. Bring the stock to a boil and add the mushrooms and spring onion whites and cover. Let the broth simmer for 4 to 5 minutes so that it absorbs the flavors of all the sauces that have been added.

Put the chicken and the green part of spring onions to blend in the broth and scoop out into bowls so as to retain the green color and crunch of the onions. Sprinkle the lemon zest you had saved along with fish sauce for personal preference.

This is one healthy and hot chicken soup that provides a really low-calorie meal and makes you want to enjoy it more often.

Recipe no. 3 – Healthy Chicken Minestrone Soup
Ingredients

½ cup oil

6 oz. onions, finely cut

2 medium cloves of garlic, crushed

6 oz. celery, sliced

4 oz. sliced carrots

2 tbsp. herb and garlic seasoning mix

8 oz. zucchini, large diced

6 oz. green beans cut in lengths

6 oz. cabbage, finely cut

½ cup white wine

8 cups of chicken stock

1 can of tomatoes or fresh tomatoes

1 whole chicken, shredded into bite-sized pieces

Salt and black pepper

How to Cook

Chop all the vegetables beforehand so that you do not have to waste any time in preparing the soup once you ready. In a big pan, heat oil and add vegetables one by one, and lower the lid to make sure they give all their flavor and are done the right way. Start with onions, carrots, garlic, and celery and add zucchini along with the seasons and stir them really well for at least a minute.

Add green beans, cabbage, wine and cover the pot. Let it cook for a few minutes. Make sure the tomatoes are cut very well before adding them to the soup so that they take lesser time to cook. Lower the heat and let the soup cook for at least 50 minutes.

Lastly, add the chicken and check out the seasoning before serving.

This soup is an excellent way to enjoy all the low carb vegetables without the added calories that pasta and beans offer. This makes a very hearty and filling meal, and you can enjoy it with bread or croutons for extra serving.

Recipe no. 4 - Low Carb Mulligatawny Chicken Soup
Ingredients

12 cups chicken broth

2 tbsp. curry powder

6 cups cooked chicken, chopped into small bite size pieces

4 cups celery root, diced or finely chopped

1/2 cup apple cider or juice

3 tbsp. sweetener

1/2 cup fresh parsley, chopped

Salt and black pepper

Instructions

Start the cooking process by combining the broth, curry powder, chicken meat, celery root and apple cider or apple juice in a big pan and bring the mixture to a boil. Let it simmer on low heat for at least 50 minutes so that all the flavors get mixed well.

Lastly, all the sweater and fresh parsley, adjust salt and pepper and serve. If you like sour cream, you can add a little after dishing out the soup in the bowl. This soup tastes best when served really hot and it is an excellent way to utilize all your left over chicken and makes up a really great tasting low carb meal.

Recipe no. 5 – Low Carb Chicken & Squash Coup
Ingredients

8 cups chicken broth

1 lb chicken breasts, chopped or shredded

2 cups chopped celery,

1 cup chopped yellow squash

2 cups chopped zucchini

1 cup chopped onions

1 cup chopped green beans,

2 teaspoon basil

2 teaspoon salt

Black pepper

Celery salt (optional)

Instructions

Put together chicken, chicken broth, celery, yellow squash, zucchini, onions and green beans along with salt and basil and let the mixture boil. All the ingredients should be covered in the broth and if needed, add water.

Let the soup simmer on the pot for at least 1 hour so that the chicken meat is very tender and the vegetables are completely done. Serve after adjusting the salt and pepper content.

Chapter 03: Low Carb Fish Soup Recipes

Fish is one of the most healthiest meats and doctors recommend a good portion of fish in our meals to avoid problems like heart diseases and enjoy natural sources of omega 3.

Recipe no. 1 - Spicy Fish and Ginger Soup Ingredients

2 tbsp. olive oil

2 medium sized fresh ginger pieces, peeled and minced

6 garlic cloves, finely chopped

3 tsp. lemon zest

1-liter chicken broth

2 tsp. fish sauce

8 big carrots, peeled and sliced thinly

1/2 tsp red pepper flakes for added flavor

1 lb filet fish

2 tsp. sesame oil

8 green onions, white and green separated and thinly sliced

½ cup chopped fresh cilantro

2 tbsp. lemon juice

Method

Heat oil in a pan and add garlic, ginger and lemon zest and cook for just a minute so that all the flavors get mixed. Add the broth and fish sauce and bring it to a boil and put in carrots too.

Let the carrots cook in the broth on a medium flame for at least 20 to 25 minutes till they are soft. Put in the fish, sesame oil and the green onions.

Cook on low flame till the fish is cooked and ready to serve which will take about 5 to 10 minutes depending on the size of the fish pieces.

The soup is ready to serve; sprinkle cilantro and lemon juice and enjoy this spicy, ginger flavored low carb soup.

Recipe no. 2 - Chunky Mediterranean fish soup
Ingredients

Tomato and basil pasta sauce (readymade variety will do)

1 liter fish stock

3 zucchini, finely sliced

2 bulb fennel, finely sliced

2 lb hoki fillet, defrosted

Handful of basil for seasoning

1 tsp chipotle chili

Preparation

Combine the pasta sauce and the fish stock in a big pan and boil them. Lower the flame and let them simmer. Put in courgettes and fennel and let them cook for a few minutes so that they are tender.

Cut the hoki fillets into small pieces and add them to the soup so that they are cooked really well. Do not stir the spoon too often in the soup as it will break the fish pieces that are already small. Once the fish is done, add the basil and check out the seasoning.

Lastly, add the chipotle chili mix or chili paste and serve.

Recipe no. 3 – Low Carb Chinese Fish Soup Ingredients

2 teaspoon canola oil

6 cloves of garlic, chopped finely

3 cups finely chopped cabbage

8 cups fish broth

2 cups mediums sized fish pieces

5 tablespoons reduced-sodium soy sauce

4 tablespoons rice-wine vinegar or distilled white vinegar

10 ounces Chinese wheat noodles

4 scallions, trimmed and chopped

Method

Heat oil in a saucepan and add garlic. Stir till it changes its colors and starts getting golden. Add the cabbage and a little broth and bring it to a boil. Cook until the vegetable is soft and then later the remaining broth, fish, soya cause and vinegar and put it on low flame.

Boil noodles in salted water until they are tender, it will only take 2 to 5 minutes. Drain them and add to the soup. The soup is ready to be served. Check out the seasoning and ladle into the bowls.

Recipe no. 4 – Low Carb Hot & Sour Fish Soup
Ingredients

2 tsp coriander seeds

1 medium piece ginger

1 liter fish stock

500 grams fish fillet cut in small pieces

250 grams thin rice noodles

4 tbsp. fish sauce

3 fat red chili, deseeded and thinly sliced

4 garlic cloves, thinly sliced

4 spring onions chopped

Handful of coriander and mint leaves

2 limes for juice

Preparation

Put the coriander seeds and ginger in a pan and add the stock. Bring it to a boil and lower the heat to simmer gently.

On the other stove, cook noodles according to the instructions given on the packet. Drain and keep warm so that they do not stick together.

Add fish sauce, chillies, and garlic to the soup and after cooking for a little while, add the fish pieces too. Let it cook for about 10 minutes till the first pieces are also cooked. Put off the stove and add spring onions, herbs and lime juice and the soup is ready to be served.

First, pour the noodles into the bowl and then pour in the soup for a great tasting and low carb meal.

Recipe no. 5 - Thai-style Fish Broth Ingredients

200g brown rice noodles

1 liter fish stock

2 tbsp Thai red curry paste

6 dried or fresh kaffir lime leaf

2 tbsp fish sauce

400g skinless fish

2 Chinese white cabbage chopped finely

Coriander leaves for serving

Method

Boil the noodles according to the guidelines given on the pack and immerse them in cold water to stop them from sticking.

Add curry paste, lime leaves, fish sauce and cold water to the stock and bring it to a boil. Let it simmer for a few minutes and then add the fish pieces. Frist cook uncovered and then cover the top and leave it for at least 5 minutes till the fish is tender.

Put in noodles and Chinese cabbage and put off the flame. Serve with coriander and you will enjoy a very delicious and low carb meal without going out the way.

Chapter 04: Low Carb Beef and Mutton Soup Recipes

Beef and mutton are very important for making new cells and living a healthy life as they contain high quality of protein. If we eat the lean meats, we can get the maximum benefits of beef and mutton and enjoy a slim and fit body as they have all the right things to support our body.

Recipe no. 1 – Easy and Simple Beef Soup Ingredients

2 pound ground beef

2 onions, diced finely

6 carrots sliced thinly

1 bay leaf

1 can frozen green beans

2 liters beef stock

1 tbsp. garlic and ginger paste

Salt and black pepper

Method

Cook beef, onions, salt and bay leaf with beef stock and ginger and garlic paste and 1-liter water till the meat is tender and smells great. Add the carrots and the green beans and let it simmer till the carrots are well done.

Check out the seasoning and serve. If you want, you can also add some chili flakes to add more flavor to the soup.

Recipe no. 2 – Low Carb Traditional Beef Soup
Ingredients

1 lbs. beef stew meat

2 cups beef broth

1 teaspoons salt

1 teaspoon pepper

1 teaspoon paprika

1 teaspoon Worcestershire

1 small yellow onion, chopped

1 tablespoon garlic, minced

2 medium carrots, cut into slices

2 medium celery sticks, cut into slices

Instructions

Sprinkle the beef with salt and pepper and leave it for a while. Cook the beef on low flame till it gets brown on all sides. Add the broth as well as paprika, Worcestershire sauce, garlic and onions and let it cook for at least 1 to 2 hours till the beef is tender.

Add carrots and celery and let it simmer for 30 to 40 minutes till the vegetables are done and enjoy a high protein, low carb meal.

Recipe no. 3 – Low Carb Mushroom Beef Broth
Ingredients

1 lb beef bones

15 cups of water

1 lb beef meat, lean portions are preferred

2 tbsp. ginger and garlic crushed

4 carrots, cut into pieces

4 celery sticks, cut into pieces

2 tbsp. soya sauce

2 tbsp. chilli sauce

1 bay leaf

Salt and pepper

Pinch of sugar

Half a can of mushrooms halved or quartered

Method

Put the beef bones to boil with water, bay leaf, soy sauce, chili sauce, salt, and pepper as well as crushed ginger and garlic. Add the meat once the broth is halfway so that the meat cooks with it and let it simmer on low heat for at least 3 hours till the meat is tender.

Strain the broth once it is ready and remove the bones. Add the meat, carrots, celery, mushrooms and sugar and let it simmer till the soup becomes thick. Check it out for seasoning and serve with crusty bread.

Recipe no. 5 – Vegetable Beef Soup Ingredients

1 pound ground beef

2 tbsp. oil

3 to 4 fresh tomatoes

4 tbsp. tomato sauce

1 pack of frozen mixed vegetables

1-liter beef broth

1 teaspoon white sugar

Salt and pepper

Method

Sauté the beef on low heat for about 5 minutes in a pan till it is all brown and no moisture remains in it. Add the tomatoes, tomato sauce, vegetables and the beef stock. Bring it to a boil on high flame; cover the lid and lower the flame to let it cook for some time.

Give it at least 30 minutes to cook and you will have a perfect low carb beef vegetable ready to serve.

Recipe no. 5 – Italian Style Beef Soup Ingredients

2 pounds ground sirloin

1/2 cup chopped onion

3 to 4 large fresh tomatoes finely chopped

10 cups water

2 tablespoon salt and pepper

1liters beef broth

4 carrots, chopped finely

4 stalks celery, chopped finely

1/4 teaspoon dried thyme

1 bay leaf

1/4 teaspoon dried basil

Method

Cook the sirloin and onion on low flame so that both are nicely brown and done. Add tomatoes, water, salt, carrots, thyme, bay leaf and basil. Let it cook on low flame till the meat starts getting tender and the liquid has reduced considerably which will take about 2 to 3 hours at least.

Add the beef broth; let it cook for at least 20 minutes to fuse the flavors and season with salt and pepper.

Chapter 05: Special Low Carb Filling Soups

Special low carb filling soup recipes have been specifically designed to help you lose weight the best way without going hungry for long periods of time and facing deficiencies that can create problems for you in the long run.

These unique low carb filling soups are the best way for you to get rid of excessive weight and enjoy delicious food that you love.

Recipe no. 1 - Tuscan Turkey Soup Ingredients

4 tablespoons olive oil

2 cup chopped onion

2 cup chopped celery

4 garlic cloves, minced

2 liters chicken broth

1 can kidney or cannellini beans

3 cups cooked turkey

1 teaspoon salt

1 teaspoon dried basil

1/2 teaspoon pepper

How to Make

Heat oil and add onion, celery, and garlic and cook for a few minutes till the vegetables are coated in the oil and begin to cook. Pour in the broth and turkey meat as well as salt, basil and peppers and let it cook on medium flame.

First let it cook uncovered, then cover the lid and lower the flame stirring after every few minutes to see how the vegetable are doing. Once all the flavors have mixed really well, the low carb turkey soup is ready to be served.

Recipe no. 2 – Garden Vegetable Noodle Soup
Ingredients

2 teaspoons minced garlic

3 tablespoons olive oil

1 cup wheat noodles

2 liters chicken broth

2 cup chopped sweet red pepper

2 cup chopped green pepper

1 cup thinly sliced fresh carrots

1 teaspoon salt

1 teaspoon dried basil

1/2 teaspoon dried rosemary, crushed

Black pepper

2 medium zucchini

How to Prepare

Fry garlic in the oil for one minute and add the noodles and cook together. Pour in the broth, peppers, carrots and seasonings and bring the mixture to a boil. Cover the pan and let it cook for about 20 to 30 minutes till the vegetables and noodles are done really well.

Lastly, add the zucchini let it simmer on low heat for 20 more minutes. Make sure the soup is served hot with lots of vegetables and it will make a appetizing meal.

Recipe no. 3 – Noodle & Chicken Soup Ingredients

1 whole chicken cut into pieces

10 cups water

1 large onion, quartered

1 cup chopped fresh parsley

1 celery rib, sliced

6 teaspoons chicken bouillon granules

6 whole peppercorns

5 whole cloves

1 bay leaf

3 teaspoons salt

1 teaspoon pepper

Dash dried thyme

4 medium carrots, cut finely

1 pack wheat noodles

Method

Add the chicken, water, onion, celery, peppercorns, chicken bouillon granules, cloves, bay leaf as well as salt and pepper and bring to a boil. Reduce the flame and cover the pot so that it cooks into a nice stock for about 2 to 3 hours.

In the meantime, boil noodles according to the instructions given on the pack and keep them in cold water.

Remove the chicken pieces from the stock and separate the meat from bones. Add chicken and carrots to the stock and also add the noodles before serving. Make sure to sprinkle parsley and dried thyme before dishing out in the bowls.

Recipe no. 4 – High Protein Low Carb Delicious Soup

Ingredients

2 large onions, chopped

4 cloves garlic

4 stalks chopped celery

400 grams frozen spinach

500g frozen green beans

3 large zucchinis, finely cut

2 leek, sliced

2 liters chicken broth

4 chicken breast cut into pieces

1   teaspoon   oregano

Salt and pepper

Tabasco sauce (to taste)

Fresh parsley

How to Cook

Put all the ingredients in a large pan and let them simmer till the vegetables and the chicken meat is tender. Take out the chicken, cut it into small pieces and return to the stock. Let it simmer for another half an hour till it is done.

Recipe no. 5 – Clear Onion and Mushroom Soup
Ingredients

4 to 5 button mushrooms, chopped

4 carrots

4 celery stalks

4 garlic cloves

2 big onions

Handful Scallions

Soy sauce and sriracha sauce to taste

Salt and pepper

1-liter cups Vegetable broth

Method

Chop all the vegetables and put them in the broth and let it simmer on low heat till the vegetables are tender and give off a nice aroma. Add the soya sauce and the sriracha sauce, along with the salt and pepper and the onion and mushroom soup is ready. Serve it with freshly chopped coriander leaves for best taste.

Part III – Low Carb Casseroles

Low Carb Casseroles are meals which are eaten to reduce weight by many people. If you are trying to lose weight then do not go on dieting plan but instead exercise and have healthy food which contains all the necessary nutrients you need. It is obvious that every ingredient cannot be eaten separately due to which there are delicious recipes for you to try. Casseroles do not have anything oily in them because they are baked and cooked under the same heat.

They are surely the perfect diet plan which you can use during the process of losing weight. You can make a casserole and keep it for 2-3 days to eat it on and off. This will be included in your weight loss plan. They are low in carbs and fat which help you get lean. No matter you like chicken, beef, vegetable or any other thing made of casserole, they are amazing to try. There are proteins in the meat whether it is white meat or red meat. Along with that, vegetables provide you the nutrients which you may miss while working out daily so gain them back but in a healthy way .

Chapter 1 – Chicken Casserole Recipes

1. *Chicken Veg. Casserole*

Ingredients:
- Chicken (boneless)
- Oil (according to your choice)
- Carrots (2)
- Onion (2)
- Seasoning (Cajun)
- Juice (Orange ¼ cup)
- Peas (as needed)
- Chicken broth
- Dill (chopped)
- Parsley

Recipe:

First of all, put the chicken in to a pot and boil the water in it. Once it is boiled, keep it aside. On the other hand, turn on the oven to 375 degrees F. Let it get warm and heat the stove, add oil as needed to the pan and add onion and carrots. Cook them until they look soft and sprinkle the seasoning of Cajun on it. Let it stay there of about 10-15 minutes.

Cook the vegetables and stir it for about 5 minutes. Add the orange juice and the broth until it boils. Add the peas and parsley and once they are cooked, pour in the buttermilk. Transfer everything to a baking pan and then place chicken on it. Let it stay in oven for about 10-15 minutes. Now, take it out and it is ready to eat!

Health Benefits:
25g Protein
13g Fat
340 Calories
30g Carbs

2.   *Chi-Broccoli Casserole*

Ingredients:

- Butter (any)
- Mayonnaise (half can)
- Mushroom soup (any brand)
- Salt and pepper according to taste
- Onion as needed
- Chicken (cooked and mashed)
- Broccoli (chopped)

Recipe:

 Spread butter on the baking dish so that it stays moist for the ingredients to stay on it. Now, heat the oven to 375 degrees Fahrenheit. While it warms up, take a bowl and stir the cream, soup and the mayonnaise together. Add salt and pepper as desired. Add the onions

in it which should be chopped with the shredded cheese. Now cover the chicken as well as the broccoli in all this mixture.

Now shift all the mixture including the chicken into the baking dish and put it in the oven for about 5-6 minutes. Now as it gets cooked, take it out and season it so that it melts in between the hot chi-broccoli casserole which you will enjoy eating.

Healthy Benefits:

3g carbs per serving

Protein 21 g

Fat 6 g

Sodium 80 mg

3.   *Chicken Mushroom Casserole*

Ingredients:

- Oil as needed

- Onion (1)

- Mushrooms (as required)

- Garlic (cloves)

- Spinach as needed

- Parsley

- Milk (2-3 cups)

- Salt and pepper to taste

- Chicken

- Almonds for seasoning

Recipe:

At first, you need to warm up the oven up to 375 degree F. Now oil the baking dish in which you are going to place the casserole. On other side, take the pan and heat it over low heat. Fry the onions which are sliced and cook them for about 6-7 minutes. Add mushrooms and let them cook as well.

Now add garlic and let it cook for about a minute. Take a bowl and transfer all of it in it. In the same pan, you need to pour milk in it as desired. As the milk warms up, take it off the heat. If you want, you can add salt and pepper as well. Now the cheese melts and you will see how smooth and soft the sauce is.

Take chicken and make it boneless. Or if you have it boneless before then it is perfect. Add the chicken into the cheese mixture and coat it all. Now, put it all into the baking dish and let it cook in oven for about 5-7 minutes. You will sense a smell that it has been cooked, now take it out and shred the almonds on it as seasoning or any other seasoning you like.

Health Benefits:
Calories 22
Total Fat 0.3 g
Carbohydrate 3.3 g

4. *The Nacho Casserole*

Ingredients:

- Chicken breast (as needed)
- Tomatoes
- Carrots
- Garlic (Cloves)
- Red Chili powder
- Cheese (Feta preferable) (low fat)
- Cilantro
- Sauce (any you like)

Recipe:

This is a quick and easy to make recipe where you have to heat the oven first at 400 degrees F. Take the baking dish and spray it over with the cooking spray. Take the bowl and mix all the ingredients along with chicken breast piece.

Take the bowl which you have sprayed and add all the mixture in it. Bake it for about 20-25 minutes in the oven and when it is done and top it up with your favorite seasoning of mint or parsley. And note, if you want you can add any kind of sauce on it.

Healthy Benefits:
Calories 23
Carbohydrate 3.7 g
Fat 0.5 g
Protein 27 g

5.   *Spicy Chicken filled Casserole*

Ingredients:

- Salsa (the main ingredient so do not miss this)
- Tomato sauce as needed
- Chipotle sauce
- Chicken chopped
- Salt and pepper as needed
- Cheese Shredded (low fat)
- Cilantro as needed

Recipe:

Heat up the oven to 400 degree F. Oil the baking dish and then add the salsa and sauces together. Pour them in separate bowl and then add the chicken into it.

Add the chicken. Put a layer of shredded cheese on chicken and cilantro as well. Do this again by making the same layer over the shredded cheese. This is how you will make the serving thicker and delicious.

Now when you are done with all the dressings, take the entire baking dish and bake it for about 20-25 minutes. Make sure to keep on checking it until it cooks properly. Once it is cooked, take it out carefully and serve it in pieces by cutting it.

Health Benefits:

Protein 27g

Vitamin A 3%

Iron 7%

Chapter 2 – Vegetable Casseroles

6.   *The Squashy Casserole*

Ingredients:

- Oil as needed, if you have a spray that would be better.
- Squash
- Onions (2)
- Cheese (shredded) (low fat)
- Salt and pepper as needed
- Pimientos (diced considered)
- Sauce (any)
- Basil
- Garlic (cloves)

Recipe:

Heat up the oven up to 350 degree F. Cover the baking dish with the oil or if you have spray then that would make it convenient for you. The whole dish should be mildly moist with the oil.

Take a pot and cook all the main ingredients in it such as onion, squash and pimientos. Make sure to cook the vegetables since you are going to keep it all in the oven to bake it at the end. Now when the vegetables are boiled, take them out of water. Add all the ingredients together and then add the salt and pepper to taste.

Take all the mixture and pour it all in the casserole baking dish. Now cook it for about 40 minutes in the oven. Keep a track of time and when it is cooked, take it out and let it cool a bit then it is ready to eat.

Health Benefits:

Fat 0.3 g

Protein 1.2 g

Calories 17

Carbohydrate 3.1 g

7.   *The Delicious Pepper Casseroles*

Ingredients:

- Peppers (3 different kinds) -   Sour Cream (low fat)
- Milk (skimmed or low fat)
- Salsa
- Cheese (low fat)
- Cilantro leaves
- Onions (cut properly in round shape)

Recipe:

Turn on the broiler of the oven and cook the peppers in it for about 10-15 minutes so that they are soft enough to be chewed. Take them out and cover them in foil. Now turn on the oven and heat it to 350 degree F. Until it warms up, take a bowl and add the sour cream and milk together. Mix it well so it takes a shape of a thick cream.

Now put the layer of the cream and milk mixture. Repeat the layers two three times more in order to make it thick.

Now, bake it for about 50 minutes in the oven and keep the heat consistent. Do not check it again and again since it cooks in the warmth of the oven. As you see the top of the meal getting brownish then it is time to take it out before it burns. You can add the cheese before baking or after it, however you like it. Spread the onions and cilantro on it to serve the dish and enjoy it.

Health Benefits:

Carbohydrates 63 g

Fat 1.2 g

Protein 21 g

8. *The Artichokes Casseroles*

Ingredients:

- Artichokes (peeled)
- Fennel
- Cream (low fat)
- Garlic (cloves)
- Nutmeg
- Salt and pepper as desired

Recipe:

Turn on the oven and heat it to 350 degree F. until it warms up, take the pot on the other side and add all the ingredients in it. Bring it to boil. Make sure they are cooked. Now reduce the heat and let them cook under the heat.

Take a baking dish and spray it with the cooking oil, add the mixture in the baking dish and cover it with the breadcrumbs. Put it in the oven for about 40 minutes and it will be ready to eat.

Health Benefits:

Fat 0.2 g

Carbohydrate 11 g

Protein 3.3 g

9.   *The Cauliflower Casserole*

Ingredients:

- Pumpkin seeds
- Butter
- Cauliflower
- Cheese (low fat)
- Mustard seeds
- Salt and pepper as taste
- Garlic (cloves)
- Half and half cream (half cup)

Recipe:

First you have to get all the vegetables together in order to bake them. Heat up the oven up to 400 degree F. Spray the baking dish so that the ingredients do not stick to it and it is easy to take it out as well after baking. Now mix all the ingredients together from the first ingredient to the end except cauliflower. You have to create layers with layering the cauliflower on the mixture. Repeat the layers 2-3 times. Now when all the mixture is ready, cook it in oven for about 30-35 minutes.

After baking you have to do the seasoning. Now when you are done, you will see the brownish toppings, so it is ready to eat!

Healthy Benefits:

Calories 25 Carbohydrate
5 g

Protein 1.9 g

10.   *The Favorite Spinach Casserole*

Ingredients:

-   Milk (low fat)
-   Cream (low fat)
-   Garlic (cloves)
-   Bay leaf
-   Salt as desired
-   Bacon (slices)
-   Spinach leaves
-   Butter as needed
-   Onions
-   Cheese (low fat)
-   Lemon juice
-   Pepper as needed (grounded)

Recipe:

Get a pan and cook the milk, cream and the bay leaf in it. On the other side, turn on the oven to 350 degrees F. Now when it has boiled, take out the milk and cream mixture aside for a while.

You have to cook the bacon slices until they look crispy. Also, in the same pan, cook the spinach lightly but make sure it does not mash in between. Add salt and pepper as of your taste. When it is down, take it out in the bowl and keep it aside to cool.

Now in the same pan, add butter and melt it. Cook the onions and garlic until they look tender to you. Put cheese and the lemon juice and stir it all. Now you have three things which are separate. You need to add all this into the baking dish and cook in the oven for about 30-40 minutes. If you wish, you can add more cheese on top of the baking dish to make it delicious. Once cooked, let it cool for 10 minutes then it is ready to serve.

Health Benefit:
Calories 23

Carbohydrate 3.6 g

Protein 2.9 g

Chapter 3 – Beef and Mutton Casseroles

11.   *Beef Casserole with Onions*

Ingredients:

- Butter
- Onions (3)
- Garlic (chopped)
- Bay Leaf (1)
- Thyme
- Mushrooms
- Oil as needed
- Steak (cut into dices)
- Salt and pepper to taste
- Beef broth
- Wine (red)
- Sauce
- Sour Cream (low fat)
- Parsley

Recipe:

Take out the pan and add the butter to melt in it. Now add the chopped onions, garlic and bay leaf in it to cook. Add salt and pepper as desired. Cook this until you see them light brown, now add the thyme also at the end, and cook it for 5 more minutes. Now, put the mushrooms and keep the heat low.

After it is cooked, take it out in a bowl and keep it separate. Now make the sauces by getting them all together and cook them for about 5 minutes. Once you are done with that, take the sour cream and mix it all together. Take the beef mixture and wash it with water. Then keep it on a low heat with the red wine in it because that helps the beef cook faster. Once it is cooked, take it off and keep it separate. Melt the cheese and spread it over the cooked beef. Mix everything together and season it with parsley. Serve it hot with buns.

Health Benefits:

Protein 26 g

Carbohydrate 0 g

Potassium 318 mg

Sodium 72 mg

12.   *Meaty Casserole*

Ingredients:

- Meatballs
- Sauce
- Cheese (low fat)
- Seasoning(any you like)

Recipe:

You can buy the frozen meatballs from the market or you can also cook them yourself. If you are someone who does not like to spend more time in kitchen then catch a pack of meatballs from the store and get started. Turn on the oven to 350 degrees F and put the meatballs to cook in the oven heat. Keep it inside for about 5 minutes. Take it out and then pour the sauces as desired. Add the cheese on the meatballs by covering it.

Bake it for about 20 minutes and it is ready to it. Do the seasoning whichever you like according to your taste.

Health Benefits:
Protein 21 g
Carbohydrate 8 g
Potassium 180 mg
Sodium 550 mg
Fat 9 g

13. *Ground Beef Casserole*

Ingredients:

- Beef
- Onion (chopped)
- Salt and pepper to taste
- Water (half cup)
- Sauce (tomato)
- Cheese (low fat)
- Mixed vegetables
- Biscuits (any)
- Butter
- Oregano

Recipe:

Heat the oven to 375 degrees F. Take out a baking dish and spray it with oil so that the ingredients do not stick to it. Take a pan and cook the beef in it so that it is not raw. When you see it cooking half way then add the onions in it which should be chopped. You can season it with salt and pepper if you want. Add the water and then add the sauce in the same pan. Let it cook for a bit until you feel that it is ready.

Now spread the entire mixture as a layer in the baking dish and cover it with cheese which should be shredded. Add the vegetables accordingly by covering the entire dish as a layer and then add cheese on it again.

Adding the crunch to it, take the biscuits and crush them. Spread them over the dish and put it oven for about 25 minutes to cook. Also when it is half way cooked, add the oregano on top of it and let it cook for another 10 minutes. You will be ready with the dish to eat at the lunch/dinner.

Health benefits:
Protein 14 g
Potassium 218 mg
Sodium 67 mg

14.   *The Cheesy Beef Casserole*

Ingredients:

- Butter
- Onion (chopped)
- Garlic (cloves)
- Mushroom
- Cream (low fat)
- Chicken
- Pepper and Salt as taste
- Beef (grounded)
- Carrots
- Cheese (slices) (low fat)

Recipe:

Heat the pan on the light heat and then melt the butter in it. Add the onion and garlic and cook it. Later on add mushrooms to it and wait until it is cooked light brownish. Cook for about a minute and then add cream and broth in it. Making it thick paste. When you think it is ready, then take it off the heat.

On the other hand, turn on the oven to 350 degrees F and spray it the oil in it. Now add the cream which you cooked, spread the beef. Make sure to combine it all in the baking dish and place it in the oven. In the middle, take it out and add cheese on it. After that cook for 10 more minutes and take it out to eat it.

Health Benefits:

Protein 18 g

Potassium 213 mg

Sodium 48mg

15.   *The Beef Noodle Casserole*

Ingredients:

- Pasta
- Beef (grounded)
- Sauce
- Garlic
- Salt and pepper as needed
- Sour Cream (low fat)
- Cheese (shredded) (low fat)
- Onions (green)

Recipe:

Turn on the oven to the heat of 350 Degree F. keep the baking dish prepared with the oil on it lightly spread. You should have pasta cooked on the other hand so that it is ready to be added to the dish. Now, cook beef in the pan so that it is fully ready when you are ready to put it in oven. Stir it and add the sauces in it as well as salt and pepper. Cook it for about 10 minutes and then let it cool.

In another bowl, add the cream and the cheese together making it a thick paste. Now combine everything in the dish and at the end pour the cream thick paste on it. Place it in the oven for about 30 minutes and you will love it once it is ready to eat!

Health benefits:

Protein 19 g
Potassium 214 mg
Sodium 49 mg

Chapter 4 – Ham Casseroles with Delicious Flavors

Ham Casserole

Ingredients:

- Noodles
- Ham
- Cheese (1 cup) (low fat)
- Cream (low fat)
- Milk (Low-Fat)
- Butter (1 teaspoon)

Recipe:

Cook the ham as they are tender. Now keep the ham in the dish with the butter on it. Mix the ham and cheese together and spread it over the casserole dish. Mix the milk and the soup of ham and create its layer on top of the mixture. Put it in oven at the heat of 375 degree F for about 30-40 minutes and it will be ready to enjoy.

Health benefits:

Protein 31 g
Fat 7 g
Carbohydrate 1.4g

Hash Brown Casserole with Ham

Ingredients:

- Cheese (low fat)
- Soup
- Cream (low fat)
- Onions (3)
- Ham (should be diced)
- Cajun for seasoning
- Butter as needed
- Salt and pepper as needed

Recipe:

This is the easiest recipe of all, all you need to do is to mix all the ingredients in the bowl and then place them in a casserole dish with mixing the ham in it. The ham should be cooked before in order for it to be tender. Place the dish in the oven for about 30 minutes and you will be done with cooking the delicious meal.

Health Benefit:

Protein 21 g
Potassium 190mg
Sodium 89 mg

Ham and cheese casserole

Ingredients:

- Onions
- Butter as needed
- Milk (half cup) (low fat)
- Sauce
- Yellow mustard
- Salt and pepper as needed
- Cheese (low fat)
- Ham, should be cooked

Recipe:

In a pan, cook the onion in the butter. Make sure that they are dried when you have cooked them. Place them in a separate plate. Make the white sauce now and blend it thoroughly. Add the salt and pepper as desired. Mix it well until it turns thick.

Now you need to get everything in the dish by creating layers. Cover the dish with the ham and then cheese over it. Then place the ham on it with cheese above it. Then cover it again with cheese layer. Bake this for 20 minutes in the oven for 350 degree F and it will be ready to serve.

Health Benefit:

Protein 21 g

Fat 6 g

Carbohydrate 1.5 g

19.   *Ham Celery Casserole*

Ingredients:

- Butter
- Celery
- Onions
- Cooked Ham
- Half and Half cream
- Salt and pepper as needed
- Nutmeg
- Cheese (low fat)

Recipe:

Turn on the oven to heat it at 350 degree F. butter the casserole dish. Take a pan and then add celery until it is tender. Further, add the onions and the ham which should be cooked before however you like it to be cooked. Mix it all well and then add the salt and pepper to taste. Also add nutmeg at the end. Mix it gently. Take it all out in a bowl and then melt the cheese in the pan for the dressing.

Now put everything in the casserole dish by placing the ham first and then the mixture. Over it, pour the melted cheese. Let it cook for about 30 minutes and when it turns light brown color, take it out and eat it with your friends or family.

Health benefit:

Protein 19 g

Fat 8 g
Carbohydrate 1.5 g

20.   *Ham Casserole with Vegetables*

Ingredients:

- Carrots
- Green pepper
- Ham Diced (cooked)
- Onion
- Celery
- Half and half cream (low fat)
- Salt and pepper to add taste
- Parsley
- Cheese (low fat)

Recipe:

Cover the dish with butter and turn on the oven to 325 degree F. Heat the flame and add butter in the pan. As it gets warm, add onion and make sure they turn soft. Add the green pepper as well as the carrots in it to be cooked. Now you can add the salt and pepper to taste as well. Cut the carrots in to slices and then make sure to cook them separately as well.

Pour all this to the baking dish and the dress it with the cheese. Cook it in the oven for about 45 minutes and check in between if the cheese is being turned brown. You will get to know when it is cooked by its delicious smell. Once cooked, it is ready to be served hot.

Health benefit:

Protein 22 g

Fat 5 g

Carbohydrate 1.9 g

Chapter 5 – Italian and Mexican Casseroles

21.   The Fajita Casserole

Ingredients:

- Sauce (tomato or any other)
- Chicken breast
- Onions
- Fajita for seasoning
- Cheese (low fat)

Recipe:

Heat the oven to 375 degrees F and take out the baking dish. Now here is a certain order which you need to follow in order to make perfect fajita casserole. Put the chicken at the bottom. Take a bowl and mix all and sauce together. Put a layer of it at the top. Now in the same bowl, take the chicken and the fajita, mix it well and put that layer on the dish. Cover it with cheese. Bake for about 30 minutes and cook it until you see the brown topping of cheese.

Health Benefit:

Protein 21 g

Fat 4 g

Carbohydrate 1.6 g

22. *Hot Jalapeno Casserole*

Ingredients:

- Spinach
- Butter
- Onion (chopped)
- Jalapeno (chopped or normal sized)
- Sour cream (low fat)
- Cumin seeds
- Cheese (low fat)
- Chicken (small pieces or sliced)

Recipe:

Wash the spinach first and then let it dry. Heat the oven to 350 degrees F and let it get warm. On the other hand, take a pan and put butter in it to melt. Now add all the main ingredients to be cooked as well as the cream to make it a thick paste. Add the cumin also accordingly.

Now put it all in the baking dish by layering on the top the chicken on it. Repeat the layers and bake it in the oven for about 45 minutes. Make sure that the cheese is melt before you take it out.

Health benefits:

Protein 21 g

Fat 5 g

Carbohydrate 1.3 g

23. *Cheese Beef Bell Casserole*

Ingredients:

- Beef
- Onion
- Garlic powder
- Tomato sauce
- Sour cream (low fat)
- Cheese (any you want) (low fat)

Recipe:

Heat the oven to 350 degree F. Take a pan and cook the beef in it. You always have to cook the beef or chicken before baking so that you get good results once the meal is fully cooked. Add onion and garlic powder into the beef mixture and put it aside when done.

Now mix the cream and the cheese to make it thick paste. After you are done with it, take the baking dish and pour both of these mixtures in it. Cover it with cheese. Put it in oven and cook it for about 20 minutes. After cooked, serve hot.

Health benefit:
Protein 19 g
Fat 8 g
Carbohydrate 1.8g
Sodium 82 mg

24.   *The Beefy Tamale Casserole*

Ingredients:

- Grounded beef
- Onion (chopped)
- Tomatoes
- Red chili powder
- Salt and pepper according to taste
- Milk (3 cups) (low fat)
- Olives (black)
- Cheese (low fat)

Recipe:

Heat the oven to 350 degree F and take out the pan. You have to make things separate in order to combine them at the end to bake. Cook the beef and add onions to it, add the tomatoes and mix it well. Make sure that the beef is cooked well otherwise it will ruin the taste of the meal.

On the other side, cook the milk and mix it well so it gets thick. Now, place everything in the dish and pour the thick paste on it. Bake it for about 30 minutes and you delicious meal will be ready.

Health benefit:

Protein 22 g

Fat 6 g

Carbohydrate 1.7g

Sodium 70 mg

25.   *Chicken Cream Casserole (low fat)*

Ingredients:

- Chicken (cooked)
- Tomatoes
- Cream (low fat)
- Cheese (low fat)

Recipe:

Heat the oven to 350 degrees F. Take a bowl and mix all the ingredients well with each other. That will be added at the end. Put the dish in the oven and cook it for about 20 minutes. When done, take it out and as a layer add more cheese. It adds the softness taste to the meal. Enjoy the delicious chicken meal!

Health benefits:

Protein 21 g

Fat 4 g

Carbohydrate 1.5g

Sodium 90 mg

Part IV – Low Carb Meals: Top-20 Quick&Easy Delicious Low Carb Recipes To Lose Weight Fast

Dieting is almost always in the news. It seems like almost every day there is a new way of dieting. Some of these diets are endorsed by celebrities and are instantly much higher profile. However, whilst different methods do work for different people, many of these diets are not sustainable in the long term and are often part of the reason that so many people ' yo-yo ' diet.

Adopting a low carb diet provides you with an opportunity to lose weight safely, ideally just a little at a time. More importantly, the low carb diet can be adopted as a long term life style; this means you can lose weight and keep the weight off.

In essence this type of diet is exactly what it says; you will minimize your intake of carbohydrates. Specifically it is necessary to avoid foods which are high in starch such as bread or pasta. These food types will be replaced with natural sources of proteins, vegetables and natural fats.

The low carb diet is not a new fad diet; it has been used for over one hundred and fifty years and there have been many success stories. With a little effort and some preparation you can easily change the food you eat and lose weight. You will also feel fitter and stronger.

Your body burns carbohydrates for energy; however, if it has more carbohydrates than it needs then it simply stores them for use in the future. When you undertake a crash diet your body will enter starvation mode; instead of using up the carbohydrate reserves in your body it will store more of them in a bid to keep you alive as long as possible. These excess carbohydrates are the cause of fat storage in the body. Fortunately, the body can also burn protein to create energy for your muscles. This means that reducing the amount of carbs you intake and increasing the amount of natural protein, will continue to give you all the energy you need; without storing excess fat or putting your body into starvation mode.

The result of this is a slow and steady loss of excess weight and the low carb approach will reduce the level of sugar and starch in your body. Without surges of energy from these artificial energy providers your body will naturally keep a more balanced level of blood sugar. This means your levels of insulin will drop and you will burn more fat. Insulin encourages the body to store fat; the more insulin you have in your body the more fat you will store. As insulin is produced in response to sugar intake it creates a circle from which it can be difficult to extract yourself.

Almost anyone can start a low carb diet; the exceptions are those who have diabetes, high blood pressure or are either pregnant or breastfeeding. These people will need to consult with their medical professional first; you may need to take extra precautions.

The following pages will provide you with a selection of recipes to help you get started in your new lifestyle. In general if you stick to foods that are less than five percent carbs you will find it much easier to stick to your new diet. It is also important to remember that there is no restriction on the amount of food you can eat; providing you stick to the low carb options.

Of course, the most effective approach to weight loss is to include regular exercise, but the low carb diet can also be a way to simply eat healthier.

Chapter 1 – 5 delicious Ways to Start the Day

Breakfast is the most important meal of the day. Eating it does more than just tell your body to start burning energy and focus on the challenges ahead. It also gives you a morale boost in the morning and a full stomach is the best way to stave off morning cravings. Feeling full will allow you to achieve much more than if you are constantly hungry.

1.   *Bacon & Eggs*

Photo made by: cyclonebill

This simple yet delicious breakfast proves that a low carb diet is possible whilst enjoying your food! You can have as many eggs as you need to fill full. Two is usually a good number for most people along with two or three strips of bacon. The bacon can be fried in a pan and the eggs can also be fried in the same oil; the bacon residual will add flavor to the eggs. To finish your breakfast and little extra flavor you can add half a dozen cherry tomatoes and some herbs. You can even season it all with a little salt or pepper.

Nutrition Info:

The recipe adheres to the principle of low carbs and high fat; it has less than one percent carbs, seventy three percent fat and twenty six percent protein. The calorie intake of this breakfast would be 272.

2.   *Goat cheese and Herb Omelet*

Photo made by: thebittenword.com

This is another breakfast recipe which includes eggs but can be made in less than ten minutes. It is a delicious way to start any day. Simply beat three eggs in a bowl and then add a few of your favorite herbs and a little salt and pepper if required. You can then place your pan or skillet on the stove and melt a small amount of butter. Once the butter is hot add the eggs and cook for three to four minutes. The omelet should be just starting to set. You can then sprinkle two ounces of crumbled goat ' s cheese on your omelet before folding it in half and continuing to cook. It should take approximately one more minute for the cheese to be melted and your omelet will be ready. Serve and enjoy!

Nutrition Info:

This breakfast contains five hundred and twenty three calories, forty three grams of fat, just three grams of carbohydrates and thirty one grams of protein. As a bonus it is also rich in calcium which is good for your bones and teeth.

3. *Low Carb Pancakes with berries*

Pancakes are a delicious way to start the day and you will be pleased to know that even on a low carb diet it is possible to start the day this way!

You will need half a pound of cottage cheese, two tablespoons of psyllium husk powder, two tablespoons of coconut oil and four eggs. You can use butter instead of the coconut oil although the oil is generally agreed to be healthier.

Simply mix all these ingredients together in one bowl until smooth. You will then need to leave the bowl for five minutes during which time the mixture will swell. You are then ready to heat a little butter or oil in your pan and pour some of the mixture in. Each pancake will take approximately three minutes before you need to flip it and repeat the process. You will need to be careful that the cottage cheese does not stick to the side of the pan!

Once you have cooked your pancakes you can add blueberries, raspberries or even strawberries to the top and even a little whipping cream if you desire!

Nutrition Info:

This breakfast is designed to create four servings; you can adjust the mixture to your tastes. It is seventy six percent fat, eighteen percent protein and just six percent carbs. This is a total of ten carbs. One serving will have 243 calories.

4.   *Ricotta and Swiss Chard Pie*

In general pies have a pastry crust; however, when choosing a low carb diet you are best to avoid flour and pastry. Therefore this recipe is completed with a sausage crust to provide the shape and an additional flavor to help you start the day the right way.

To make this you will need to heat one tablespoon of olive oil in a pan and add half a cup of chopped onion and a clove of minced garlic. This has softened add eight cups of Swiss chard. You can use spinach if you prefer. Once the green have also softened you will need to add a pinch of nutmeg and a little salt and pepper. You can then place this to one side to allow it to cool.

Next, in a separate bowl beat three eggs together and add a cup of grated mozzarella and a quarter cup of parmesan. You will also need to add two cups of ricotta cheese. Now mix the two bowls together thoroughly.

To make the pie you will need to roll your some sausage meat, alternatively you can make small, individual pies by lining a tray with the sausage meat. Then simply pout the mixture into the mold or molds and cook for thirty five minutes on 350 degrees Fahrenheit.

The beauty of this recipe is, once cooked, you can easily take these with you; this is particularly handy if you need breakfast on the move.

Nutrition Info:

The mixture should make eight muffins / small pies. Each one will have approximately 344 calories, twenty seven grams of fat, four grams of carbs and twenty three grams of protein

5.   *Almond Minute Muffin*

Photo made by: Oonhs

This recipe is perfect for when you are in a rush. Simply mix one quarter cup of almond meal flour quarter cup of baking powder, a pinch of salt and half a teaspoon of cinnamon in a large coffee mug. Then add one egg and a teaspoon of vegetable oil before placing in the microwave on high for one minute. Then simply enjoy!

Nutrition Info:

The recipe contains twelve grams of protein, twenty three grams of fat and just four and a half grams of carbs. It is also just 279 calories!

Chapter 2 – 5 Snacks to Help You Through the Day

Ideally your balance meals should be satisfying enough to carry you through the day. However, there will always be times when you need a little extra; either through hunger or as a morale boost. In fact, many diets recommend more small meals per day and less large meals as they believe that this helps the body regulate and balance its hormones and energy demands. In truth, it is what works best for you and your lifestyle. The following recipes should help you get through any snack craving part of the day.

6.   *Pizza*

This recipe is quick and easy to make. It offers a handy snack or can even be used as part of your main meal if required! The beauty of this is that, once it has been made, it will do two or three snack times or you can share it with your friends.

To make the base you simply put some grated mozzarella into a pan and cook it on a medium heat until it bubbles. This creates a fantastic alternative to the traditional pizza base. Then simply spread some tomato puree onto the base and add your preferred topping, pepperoni is an excellent choice for this. You can also add a few seasoning such as peppers or spinach and any other flavor which appeals. Once you have created your masterpiece continue heating it in the pan until the base is bubbling and the edges are going brown. Then serve and eat hot or cold!

Nutrition Info:

This recipe contains less than one percent carbs, seventy percent fat and twenty nine percent protein; although this will depend upon the topping you use. One slice of the pizza contains just less than two hundred calories and tastes delicious!

7.   *Alternate Crisps*

Crisps are full of carbohydrates and can often be a difficult item to give up and to find a good substitute for. Fortunately there are other options! One of the best ones uses just pepperoni and can be ready in just a few minutes.

You will need a bag of sliced pepperoni or you can slice your own pepperoni. You will also need several paper towels. Scatter the sliced pepperoni across the paper towels without allowing them to overlap. Once you have enough for your snack, cover the pepperoni with an extra piece of paper towel and place them in the microwave. They should only need heating for one minute on full power although you may need to extend this time for lower power microwaves. They should be crispy. You can eat them by themselves or with a low carb dip.

Nutrition Info:

These are excellent for anyone on the low carb diet as they have zero carbs, just 80 calories in a 17 piece serving and four grams of fat. Even better, they have an impressive nine grams of protein.

8.   *Keto Breadsticks*

Bread is a definite no when adopting the low carb diet. It is full of carbohydrates and starch. However, it is also delicious and often difficult to replace. Fortunately these breadsticks are made with almond flour, flax meal and coconut flour. The following recipe will make twenty breadsticks; one serving is considered to be four breadsticks and consists of sixteen grams of carbs, thirteen grams of protein and twenty seven grams of fat. Its calorific count is 334.

Simply mix one cup of almond flour with half a cup of flax meal and half a cup of coconut flour. You can then add in two tablespoons of psyllium husks and two tablespoons of chia seeds. Knead the mixture together with a little water if it is too dry. You can then leave the dough in the fridge for fifteen minutes.

When you are ready to remove the dough put your oven onto 350 Fahrenheit and split the dough into four pieces. Each of those pieces can then be divided into five bits which are rolled out to form breadsticks. You may need to wet your hands to roll the dough.

Nutrition Info:

The breadsticks can then be placed onto a greased oven tray. Sprinkle a little cheese on top or seeds of your choice to add extra flavor and cook for fifteen minutes until golden.

9.   *Cauliflower Cheese toastie!*

Instead of making a toasted sandwich with carb heavy bread you can opt for this low carb alternative.

To make this tasty snack you will need to pull the florets from you cauliflower and mash them up as small as possible. In the process you need to remove any excess water from the pan. The less moisture the better! You can then spread the mixture out onto grease proof paper and make your ' bread slices ' . They can be any shape you like!

These cauliflower bread slices need to go in an oven at 420 Fahrenheit for fifteen minutes until they are just turning golden.

Nutrition Info:

Once they have cooled you will be able to handle them in the same way as bread. Simply fill them with cheese and heat in a pan, turning half way through. The simply enjoy. One serving of this will provide 374 calories, twenty nine grams of fat, eight grams of carbs and twenty three grams of protein.

10. The New Hot Dog

You may have thought hot dogs were no longer an option. However, this recipe will allow you to enjoy this delicious snack any time you want and stick to your low carb diet!

To create these you will need to heat your oven to 400 Fahrenheit. Whilst it is warming you should place one and a half cups of mozzarella with two tablespoons of cream cheese in a microwaveable bowl and heat for approximately one minute; until the cheeses has melted. You will need a second bowl to mix one cup of almond flour, one egg and one teaspoon of xanthan gum. You can then add the melted cheese mix to the bowl and mix thoroughly. It should then take on the texture of dough.

You can now split the dough mixture into quarters and roll each one out. Each piece of dough can then be wrapped around a sausage of your choosing. You can then finish by beating one egg and brushing it onto the bagel. This can then be dipped into spices, herbs or even seeds to create a fantastic looking and tasting alternative hot dog. It will need to be cooked for approximately twenty minutes.

Nutrition Info:

One hot dog will contain 474 calories, thirty nine grams of fat, twenty seven grams of protein and nine and a half grams of carbohydrates.

Chapter 3 – 5 Tantalizing Lunch Options

Lunch can be an exciting time on the low carb diet, there are many options to help keep you filled up for the day ahead and away from any high carb snacks.

11.   *Greek Chicken Salad*

You do not need a Greek chicken for this delicious and healthy salad option! To create this start by mixing half a cup of red wine vinegar with two tablespoons of olive oil and a tablespoon of oregano. You will also need to add a teaspoon of garlic powder and a pinch of salt and pepper into the mix.

Once this is thoroughly mixed add six cups of your chosen lettuce, three cups of cooked chicken, chopped cucumber, half a chopped red onion, half a cup of black olives and half a cup of feta cheese. Toss the entire mixture to ensure your salad is coated with the dressing and then serve.

Nutrition Info:

This recipe will provide you with 343 calories, eighteen grams of fat, eleven grams of carbohydrates and thirty one grams of protein.

12.   *Butternut Soup*

Although this is a butternut recipe you can use any type of winter squash. Start by cutting your squash in half; you will need about one and a half pounds of squash. The seeds need to be removed from your two halves. These can then be placed onto a baking tray with the cut side on the tray. These should be cooked for approximately forty five minutes on 350 Fahrenheit; or until they are tender.

You can then scoop the insides out ready to cook with. You will need to heat a little oil in a pan and then add two stalks of chopped celery, one finely chopped small onion and a carrot; also chopped. After approximately eight minutes this should be soft and you will be able to add the insides of your squash. You can also add a teaspoon of cumin and some ground cloves; according to your taste preferences.

After cooking for approximately twenty minutes the vegetables should be soft; you can then put the hot mixture into a blender and blend until it is smooth. You can then add salt and pepper to taste and even drizzle some plain yoghurt over the top when serving.

Nutrition Info:

One serving should give you 49 calories, ten grams of carbs, twelve grams of protein and ten grams of fat.

13. *Honey Soy Salmon*

Fish is an excellent source of several important nutrients, particularly omega three oils. It can also be a delightful addition to your low carb diet.

To start you will need to whisk one scallion with two tablespoons of soy sauce, one of rice vinegar and one tablespoon of honey. You can also add a teaspoon of ginger powder. Separately place a one pound piece of salmon in a sealable plastic bag. It is advisable to cut the salmon into four pieces before you bag it. Add three tablespoons of your mixture to the bag and close it. It should be left in the fridge fro fifteen minutes.

Once it has been marinated you can place the salmon in a pan and broil it; keeping it six inches from the heat source. It should take approximately, eight minutes to cook through. You can then serve the salmon drizzled with more of the sauce that you made and add a garnish of sesame seeds. It is best served with a selection of vegetables.

Nutrition Info:

Each serving should have 160 calories, five grams of fat, six of carbohydrates and twenty three grams of protein.

14. *Stuffed Portobello's*

This low carb option is even okay for vegetarians. Providing you like Portobello mushrooms you will love the delicate flavors balanced in this dish.

You will need at least four good sized Portobello mushrooms. Scoop out their insides and spray their tops with oil. They can then be placed on a greased baking tray.

Next, you will need to put a teaspoon of olive oil in a separate pan with two cups of spinach, three cloves of garlic and half an onion. All of these need to be chopped finely. Half a chopped red pepper also adds an extra bit of flavor. Keep this on the heat for several minutes and it will go soft. You can then add four large basil leaves and keep cooking. After a while they will wilt and soften.

You will then need another bowl to mix three quarters of a cup of ricotta with half a cup of grated parmesan and one egg. Once this has been mixed you can merge the two bowls of ingredients and stuff the mixture inside the mushrooms. Finally, top the mushrooms with a little marinara sauce and some mozzarella cheese. They will take approximately twenty five minutes to cook before you can enjoy them.

Nutrition Info:

The recipe makes four servings and each one has 236 calories, thirteen grams of carbs, thirteen grams of fat and twenty grams of protein.

15. *Mexican Casserole*

This is a simple dish to make and uses cauliflower to create a base as did the grilled cheese toasties earlier. To create this delicious dish you will need to heat your oven to 350 Fahrenheit. Whilst this is warming you can place a pan with a little oil on the stove and bring to a medium heat. Then place half a chopped white onion in the pan along with a sliced red pepper, one sliced green pepper and a teaspoon of cumin as well as one of chili powder. Roast the peppers stirring the mix at least every two minutes.

Separately you will need to mash one head of cauliflower and then microwave for one minute. This should remove most of the moisture. You can then add a cup of cheese and eight chopped cherry tomatoes. Once this is blended add the mixture from the pan.

You can then add the entire lot to a baking pan and top with some grated cheese. Then cook in the oven for thirty minutes; the cheese will gradually melt.

Nutrition Info:

Assuming you split this into twelve servings then each piece will have approximately 70 calories, three grams of carbs, five grams of protein and three grams of fat.

Chapter 4 – 5 Tasty Dinner recipes

Dinner is one of the meals that many people cheat on because they have had a long day and simply want to rest. Fortunately you can create several delicious meals quickly and easily whilst sticking to your low carb diet:

16.   Chicken & Chive

To make this delicious feast you will need to have half an hour spare. Start by wrapping four boneless chicken breasts between sheets of plastic and flatten them with a meat hammer. You should make them all about half an inch thick. You can then sprinkle a little salt onto both sides of your chicken pieces.

Next you will need to place a tablespoon of oil in a pan and put it on a medium heat. Once the oil is hot, add the chicken and cook until they are a golden color; this should take a couple of minutes per side. These can then be removed from the pan and kept warm. You can then add another spoon of oil to your pan and two chopped shallots. Within a couple of minutes these should also be a golden brown color. Can then add half a cup of red wine, one can of reduced sodium broth and bring the mixture back to the boil.

You will then need to reduce the heat and add the chicken back into the mix. This should be cooked for approximately six minutes to finish cooking the chicken. You can then add half a cup of sour cream and a tablespoon of mustard. Mix it all together thoroughly and then serve garnishing with chopped chives. Add some green beans and cauliflower and enjoy!

Nutrition Info:

Each serving contains 295 calories, twelve grams of fat, ten grams of carbohydrates and twenty six grams of protein.

17.   *Macaroni Less Cheese!*

It is possible to enjoy a dish of macaroni cheese without the carb heavy pasta! This recipe is also incredibly easy to make and extremely tasty. Simply boil one cauliflower head, broken into pieces until it is soft and ready to eat.

Next, heat three tablespoons of butter in a pan over a medium heat. Then ass one small finely chopped onion. You can also add a clove of minced garlic if you want. After one minute add two tablespoons of coconut flour and stir the mixture constantly until it goes brown. Then add one can of coconut milk and half a teaspoon of mustard. You can add salt if required.

Next add two cups of grated cheddar cheese and the already cooked cauliflower. Return to a low heat and stir until the cheese is melted and it is thoroughly mixed. Add to an oven suitable dish.

You can add a topping of two tablespoons melted butter mixed with two tablespoons of flaxseeds and a quarter of a cup of parmesan.

Then cook on 400 Fahrenheit for thirty minutes, serve with vegetables and enjoy.

Nutrition Info:

One serving will have 376 calories, thirty grams of fat, seventeen grams of protein and just fourteen grams of carbohydrates.

18. *Broccoli Pasta*

Of course, this recipe does not use actual pasta, but it is as fast to make and just as delicious as eating pasta.

Add a pan with a little oil in to a medium heat stove. You can then place four cups of broccoli slaw into the pan and cook it until all the water has evaporated. This should take approximately five minutes. You will then need to add one can of crushed tomatoes, two tablespoons of parmesan cheese and a pinch of garlic, salt, pepper, and onion powder; according to your tastes.

Continue cooking on the stove for several minutes until it is all piping hot. Then serve and top with a little extra parmesan.

Nutrition Info:

Each serving will have just 134 calories, two grams of fat, seven grams of protein and two grams of carbs.

19. *Squash and Meatballs*

This delightful meal is made with two medium to large sized spaghetti squashes. The best squashes will have smooth skin.

Each of the squashes will need to be pierced five times around the centre of the vegetable. It then needs to be microwaved for three minutes; you will need to turn it over half way through.

Once heated you should be able to cut each squash in half with a good knife. You will also need to remove all the seeds from the inside before placing them, cut side up, on a baking tray. You can then coat the squash lightly in olive oil and add a little salt and pepper to taste. It will then need to go into the oven for approximately fifty minutes on 400 Fahrenheit.

You will now need to let it cool for approximately ten minutes before scrapping the insides out with a fork. This will look like spaghetti. You can then add your own home made meatballs or simply use some shop purchased ones; being careful to check the carb content of the ones you buy.

The meatballs can be topped with some marinara sauce and grated mozzarella and then grill for five minutes until hot and the cheese has melted.

Nutrition Info:

Each serving contains just 42 calories and ten grams of carbs plus the content of your meatballs.

20. *Sundried Tomato Cous Cous*

The final selection in the tantalizing dinner range uses cauliflower to mimic cous cous; it does a surprisingly good job!

You will need one cup of sun dried tomatoes which can be soaked in water to rehydrate them. Whilst this is happening place the head of a cauliflower into your blender and use the pulse setting to make it appear like couscous.

Next, saut é two minced cloves of garlic with a cup of sliced leeks and a tablespoon of grape seed oil. The rehydrated tomatoes can be chopped and added to the pan after a few minutes. After several more minutes the leeks should be soft.

Now add your cauliflower and gently heat. Do not overdo this stage as the cauliflower will go mushy! You can add a little salt and pepper for flavor if required whilst warming.

Serve with a selection of vegetables or even some pepperoni crisps to add a little meat to the mix!

Nutrition Info:

Each serving will contain approximately 326 calories, ten grams of fat and eight grams of carbs. You should also get fifteen grams of protein although these figures will vary depending upon what you serve this delicious cous cous with!

Conclusion

The weight loss is not easy, and if you want to shed some pounds, it is important to focus on a healthy diet and exercise routine. It will prove helpful to develop lean muscles for a smaller body. It can be boring for you to follow a regular exercising routine; therefore, you can try some dance steps, music and other activities to make your work interesting. Control your diet by decreasing sugar, extra sodium and fat.

Set up a workout routine for you to get rid of extra fat and maintain a good shape of your body. Regular exercise can help you to get rid of additional body fat. The use of fitness tracker will help you to record the results of our efforts. It is important to change your lifestyle gradually to avoid its any disadvantage on your body.

Eating a low carb diet on the regular basis is a great way for you to get rid of excessive fats in the body that make you look dull and lethargic. All you need to do to look slim and smart and lose weight without running into any trouble is to adopt a low carb diet that will provide you a chance to enjoy great food without going hungry for hours.

This ebook has been designed keeping in mind the needs of people who work hard all day long and look forward to a healthy and hearty meal at the end of the day but do not want to put on weight with loaded foods. Go through the ebook and try out our most delicious and easy to make low carb soups that help you stay fit very efficiently.

You must understand that it is you and only you who can play a vital role in staying healthy and all you need to achieve this goal is to cut down all the unnecessary starches and sugars from your diet and incorporate healthy vegetables and lean meats that carry proteins. This will help you achieve your ideal body weight, and you will be able to reduce fat from your body that makes it look so bad.

There are several food types which it is important to avoid as part of your new lifestyle. These include sugar, gluten grains, Trans fats, high omega 6 seed and vegetable oils, artificial sweeteners and all diet or low fat products. Although many recipes are created from fresh ingredients it is possible to cheat on several recipes and use pre-prepared items. Although this is not the recommended approach it is something that most people find necessary at some point simply due to time constraints and busy lives. The important thing to remember when purchasing any food item is to read the label and check the amount of carbs. Many products are high in carbs; you can sabotage your diet in no time!

You may hear the low carb diet referred to as a keto diet; although they are not exactly the same thing many people on a low carb diet end up on a keto diet. A keto diet has this name as eating more protein and fat than carbs forces the body into a state of ketosis. This is when the body goes into starvation mode as a response to a reduction in the amount of food being absorbed. As the body is used to using glucose from high carb food it has to go through a process of change. This is achieved by burning ketones instead of glucose; ketones are created by burning fats stored in the liver. You can enter a ketonic state by consuming less than thirty grams of fat a day and this can be beneficial for weight loss although it is not recommended as a healthy long term eating pattern. A general low crab approach is healthy and will help you to feel better as well as have more energy.

It is best to eat as much fresh meat and fish as possible as this is generally high in protein and low in carbs. Eggs, vegetables and most fruit are also good choices when living a low carb lifestyle. You will also benefit from consuming high fat dairy products, buts and seeds and even butter, coconut oil or olive oil.

Thank you for downloading this ebook, and we hope that you enjoyed reading it and are tempted to try out some of our great recipes that have been put together by health experts who know what you need to look perfect!

If you have any questions for me, I will be glad to answer them for you regarding our recipes as well as how you can achieve your perfect weight without giving up food.

CPSIA information can be obtained
at www.ICGtesting.com
Printed in the USA
BVHW052338010621
608544BV00009B/2799